Hold On To Hope
Black Saturday, My Story

Bronwyn Wakelin

First published by We Inspire Now Books 2022

Copyright © 2022 Bronwyn Wakelin

ISBN
Print: 978-0-6453052-5-8
Ebook: 978-0-6453052-6-5

Bronwyn Wakelin has asserted her right under the Copyright, Designs and Patents Act 1988 to be identified as the author of this work.

Antoinette Pellegrini, as publisher through her business, *We Inspire Now Books*, specifically disclaims responsibility for any adverse consequences, which may result from the use of the information contained herein. The author takes responsibility for the content and for any permissions to use information. Any breaches will be rectified in further editions of the book.

All rights reserved. No part of this publication may be reproduced, stored in or introduced into a retrieval system, or transmitted in any form, or by any means (electronic, mechanical, photocopying, recording or otherwise) without the prior written permission of the author. Any person who commits any unauthorised act in relation to this publication may be liable to criminal prosecution and civil claims for damages. Enquiries should be made through the publisher.

Cover image and design :   Samuel Wakelin

Editor   Antoinette Pellegrini

Layout and typesetting: Antoinette Pellegrini
                                              We Inspire Now Books

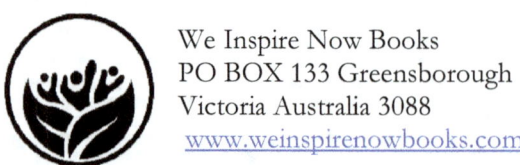

We Inspire Now Books
PO BOX 133 Greensborough
Victoria Australia 3088
www.weinspirenowbooks.com

Dedication

This book is dedicated to:

My Dad who was my greatest encourager and friend.

I also want to acknowledge:

My wonderful husband, who has been my greatest support.

My two boys, Jordan and Samuel, who have brought me such joy, and my wonderful daughters-in-law, Taleisha and Madison.

Also, all the family and friends who have stood by us and who encouraged me to write my story.

Most of all, I want to acknowledge my Lord and Saviour, Jesus, who always has shown His faithfulness in my life.

Prologue

What an absolute honour, privilege and blessing to read Bron's story.

Having known Bronwyn for some time, I am both in awe and inspired by her story of which family, community, and connection to God play a crucial role.

It is these things that have seen Bron through the darkest of times, and guided her path of service to others, even through sadness and trauma. Further, it is with this experience that enables Bron to develop meaningful connections with others in a way that enriches the lives of those around her.

Bron's story is one that takes you through a myriad of emotions, including indescribable pain and anguish, yet there is undeniable realisation that it is through connection, whether to family, community, God, or all three combined, that we really can get through the worst of disasters to live the very best of lives.

Bron is not only a truly remarkable person, but also a person who humbly inspires others to put the best of themselves forward.

Melanie Harris-Brady

Hold On To Hope
Black Saturday, My Story

Bronwyn Wakelin

Chapter 1

The Lead Up

It has been called Black Saturday, and it is such an appropriate description of the day that changed our lives forever.

The day was Saturday the 7th of February 2009. It was so hot, 42 degrees, and very windy. I drove across the top of the mountain to pick up my oldest son Jordan from the Mitre10 hardware store at 2 pm, where he was finishing his shift. The threat of fire in summer was always there at Kinglake, with the bush tinder dry, but on a day like today, with very high temperatures and high winds, the threat was more real.

As I looked across towards Melbourne, there was a huge black cloud of smoke blocking the view of Melbourne. I remember feeling worried as it felt so ominous.

Life was normal in the weeks that led up to that fateful day. It was summer, so we were experiencing hot days. As a family, we would make day trips to the beach or go to Warburton to cool off in the river. I enjoyed summer.

Many news reports were saying that we were in the worst weather conditions for bushfires, but we weren't alarmed; we had heard this before. Friends had asked us if we would leave home for the day, just in case. Darren's response was, 'Do we pack up our things and leave for the beach every time we hear reports that it will be a bad day?' The answer was, 'No.'

The week prior to Black Saturday, I was doing my regular shifts at the Austin Hospital, Darren had his IT business, and he worked from home. Jordan and Samuel had just started their first week back at school. Jordan was away at a study camp for year 12 in the city, and Samuel was in his first week of grade Five at Plenty Valley Christian College. Life was going along normally.

On the Wednesday of that week, news reports were saying it was going to be appalling weather conditions on Saturday the 7th of February. Again, nothing we hadn't heard before. It was reported that a significant heat wave was affecting the Southeast of Australia.

From the 28th to the 30th of January, Melbourne had broken temperature records of three consecutive days above 43 degrees Celsius, with temperatures getting up to 45.1 degrees Celsius on the 30th of January. This was the third hottest day in the city's history. On the 7th of February, Victoria, including Melbourne, recorded the highest temperature since records began in 1859.

On the 6th of February, the Premier of Victoria issued an extreme weather warning on the news for Saturday the 7th of February 2009. He said, 'It's just as bad a day as you can imagine, and on top of that, the state is tinder dry. People need to exercise real common sense tomorrow.' It was expected to be the worst day in the history of the State. We were unaware that 358 firefighters from the Country Fire Authority (CFA) and the Department of Sustainability and Environment (DSA) had been deployed across the state on Friday evening, the 6th of February, in anticipation of the extreme weather conditions the next day.

On Saturday the 7th of February, hot North westerly winds blew over 100kms per hour. The temperature had reached 46.4 degrees Celsius in the afternoon, the hottest temperature ever recorded in the city. Humidity levels had dropped to 2%. These were weather conditions for a perfect storm. Around midday, wind conditions were reaching their peak. A SWER line had fallen in Kilmore East, sparking a fire that would become known as the deadliest and most intense fire storm experienced in Australia post-1788 history.

We were unaware that fires had been sparked across the entire state, and it was soon coming for us.

Chapter 2

What Seemed Like A Normal Day

It was to be a fateful day. Driving up to meet my son Jordan, I did feel an ominous dread in the pit of my stomach, but I had no idea of what was to come. When I arrived at Mitre10, I asked Jordan if they had heard anything about the fire coming near us because it didn't look or feel right to me. He reassured me that the radio was saying it was heading away from us and that it was the smoke from the Kilmore fire. He said that all fire hoses and fire pumps were sold out, but he said I didn't need to worry.

When we arrived home, I told my husband Darren about the menacing black cloud obscuring our view of Melbourne and that I felt something was wrong. He reassured me that the internet and radio were saying the fire was nowhere near us, and I didn't have to worry. So I relaxed a little.

We were having my cousins over for a BBQ dinner, so I prepared salad and put the roast pork on the barbecue. They rang around 4 pm to say that they probably shouldn't come up due to the closeness of the fires to Whittlesea, where they lived. I reassured them, 'Don't worry. It's safe up here, but if you feel that it's best if you don't come, then you shouldn't. We can have the roast pork for lunch after church tomorrow'. We agreed that roast pork after church sounded good, and we all continued to relax in our air-conditioned houses.

The power went off around 5 pm. Darren fell asleep on the brick floor because it was cool. My youngest son Samuel and I were lying on the couch as he showed me the game he was playing on his Game Boy. Jordan had been playing his guitar and fell asleep on his bed. No power meant no TV and no air conditioner. When the power went off, I remember saying to Darren, 'At least we can still eat dinner because the pork is cooking on the barbecue outside, and the salads are already prepared and in the fridge.'

We lit candles for light because we were used to the power going out in Kinglake. Everything in our house ran on electricity, and because of this, we couldn't get water up to the house because it was pumped by an electric pump. No electricity also meant that we were no longer able to track the fire's progress on the Internet via the computer.

We weren't panicking because it wasn't the first time we had experienced fires in the area. We had fires in the area in January 2006.

It had been a hot January, and we had just arrived home from a weekend away in Lorne, enjoying family time away at the beach. We hadn't really been watching any news while we were away. Fires had been burning in Kinglake for the previous week, started by lightning strikes and my friend Cornelia, who lived in Kinglake Central, about five km from our house, had been monitoring the progress of the fires that she could see from her house.

We arrived home on the Tuesday just before Australia Day on Thursday the 26th of January 2006. Samuel and I had headed down to Greensborough to do grocery shopping, unaware of the closeness of the fires. We ran into another family from Kinglake West, and they informed us of what was happening. Darren had been trying to phone me to get me to come home, and of course, he couldn't get in contact with me because my phone was in my bag and I couldn't hear it. When I finally checked it, I had all these missed calls from him, and when I called him back, he told me to come straight home.

As I drove up the St Andrews road, I could see visible thick smoke, and the smell of smoke was very strong, so panic started to set in as I got closer to home.

Darren had been monitoring the fire on the computer, so he knew it had been burning for days. He got us to pack up all the important items, such as photos, passports, important documents, and hard drives that had backups from his computer, just in case we needed to evacuate.

The wind was getting stronger by the minute, and at about 4 pm, my friend Cornelia rang to say that she could see the flames from her house, and we needed to leave as the fire was predicted to take out the Kinglake township.

Anxiously I told Darren we needed to phone my mum and dad, who lived in Korumburra, to let them know what was happening and that we may need to go there. Darren said he didn't feel we needed to panic and evacuate just yet, and we would just keep monitoring the situation. It was a very sleepless night and was spent praying for God's protection over our lives and the lives of all those in Kinglake. At one stage, the wind stopped, and it was utterly still. We walked out into our backyard, and the smoke had settled low to the ground like a thick fog, and it was extremely eerie.

When morning broke, I said to Darren that I believed we needed to go, and I rang mum and dad to tell them we were coming. The boys and I packed the car, and Darren said he would follow us in his car with our boat on the back. He was just going to put his motorcycle in the house, lock it up, and then he would follow. As we were backing out the driveway, Darren was standing at the front door and informed me that he was staying to protect the house for as long as possible. He assured me that he would leave if there was an evacuation order. I felt sick, tears running down my cheeks as I drove away with the boys. There was nothing I could do to change his mind; I just had to get the boys to the safety of Mum and Dad's place.

The next few hours were excruciating as I listened to the radio reports and spoke intermittently with Darren on the phone. He had gone up to the CFA shed and the police station to find out what was happening and to let them know he was still at home

The wind was getting stronger, and the reports said that if people were going to leave, they needed to leave now. I rang Darren in a panicked state and begged him to leave now, which he finally agreed to. He had been tracking the weather on his computer and said it was amazing, there was a small cloud at first, which was getting bigger, and it was right over Kinglake. The wind changed direction, and as he was driving down the road, it began to rain.

Another answer to prayer. I prayed for the Lord's hand of protection over our lives and our property. This time our house was spared. We had time to get important items packed up, and extra clothes in suitcases. Little did we know that only three years later, we would be running for our lives, and everything we owned would be destroyed.

Our house before Black Saturday.

Our old kitchen.

Chapter 3

The Fire Arrives

So, waiting for the pork roast to cook, we were concerned but not panicked.

Around this time, I noticed a lot of movement of cars driving past our house but didn't think anything of it. Around 6 pm, everything went black. I had gotten up from the couch to check on the roast and looked across to the house across the road and saw fire behind it.

I yelled out to Darren that there was a fire across the road behind our neighbour's place, and we needed to call 000 because the wind was so strong that the fire would spread quickly. Darren jumped up and ran across the road because we saw that our neighbour was still inside. I got the boys moving and was fixed on the fire across the road, and totally unaware of what was happening behind us.

I asked Jordan to get blankets while Samuel and I were in my walk-in-robe grabbing photo albums, using his Game Boy as a torch. In my panicked state, all I thought about was grabbing our photos because they couldn't be replaced. I hadn't even thought about getting the videos that we had taken of the boys since they were born. There was no thought of anything else at the time.

We were totally unprepared for the rapid escalating disaster that was unfolding. We did not have provisions like bags packed with clothes or bottled water. This fire had taken us completely by surprise in the speed and ferocity in which it came. I was in a totally panicked state, desperate to see Darren return, so he could take charge of the situation. I told the boys we were going to lay on the brick floor and cover ourselves with blankets until the firefront passed over us.

Jordan took charge (only 17 years old at the time) and said, 'Mum, we have to go. We can't stay here.' And he proceeded to get the car keys. He told Samuel to grab anything he wanted to take out of his room. Jordan already had a bag full of clothes ready to go because he had just returned from a school study camp and hadn't unpacked his bag as I had asked him to.

Jordan was moving us towards the door when I said to him, 'Dad isn't back from across the road, and we

The Fire Arrives

aren't supposed to drive when there is fire. Also, if we start reversing down the driveway in this blackness, we won't see him and might run him over' But we didn't have to wait long as, in the next minute, Darren burst through the front door yelling, 'We need to go, get in the car.'

When we came out of the front door, I had to walk out of the carport to get into the passenger side of the car, and that was when I saw huge fireballs the size of basketballs hitting the bushes in my garden. I felt a prickly sensation on my arms and legs, and as I looked around us, it was raining fire. The air itself was on fire all around us.

As I got in the car, I realised that I needed my handbag. I always kept it in the same spot in my bedroom, so it was easy to find. Darren and Jordan went back inside to get it. I was unaware at the time that the fire was already engulfing the back of our house and that Darren's office at the side of the house had already been destroyed.

Darren ran into the kitchen to get his wallet, phone and puffer from the top of the fridge where he always kept it. The Ventolin puffer would be needed later in the night. They told me later that they had blown out the candles and locked the door behind them. We always automatically blew out the candles so a fire wouldn't start. You do strange things under pressure.

As we reversed out the driveway, the full extent of what we were dealing with came into view. The conifers that were near the top of the driveway were exploding into flames. A massive wall of fire was behind our house. The flames were hundreds of feet high, higher than the huge mountain ash trees on our boundary. I remember hyperventilating, saying, 'We are going to die!', and Darren nearly having to knock me out to stop me from losing all control. I have never felt so much fear.

We turned right out of our driveway onto Glenburn Rd, and then at the intersection at the top, we debated which way we should turn, left towards St Andrews or right towards Kinglake West. There was so much confusion, people were running, and cars were everywhere. The petrol station had just exploded into flames, so we turned right towards the football oval.

It was so black that even though we had our headlights on, we couldn't see past the windshield. Darren just had to drive by feel as the fire was all around us the entire time, engulfing our car. Darren felt it was getting too dangerous as we didn't have any idea where we were, so he decided to turn around and go back the way we had come.

We didn't get far because in the meantime a tree had fallen across the road and a motorbike and cars had crashed into it. We were still completely engulfed in fire; Jordan and I just prayed the whole time. When we saw a motorcycle down on the road, I remember saying, 'What's a motorcycle doing out in this fire, and where is the rider?'

Suddenly a man was banging on our car side window. His arms and hands were on fire. Without hesitation,

The Fire Arrives

Jordan opened his door and pulled the man inside, dowsing the flames with his hands as he pulled the stranger in. As the car door opened, you could feel the oxygen being sucked out of the car.

The man was crying, saying what I thought was, 'My wife and kids are in the car over there'. I went to open my door and run across to them, only to have Darren hold onto me and say, 'If you open that door, we are all going to die.' And with that, he turned the car around and headed back towards the football oval.

I felt physically sick knowing that his wife, and possibly children, were still in the car across the road. All I could do was pray for their protection, listening to the anguished cries of our passenger as we drove away. We later found out that he was saying his wife and dogs were in the car.

Still, we were driving through the flames, more trees had fallen across our path, but it was as if the car was being catapulted over the fallen trees. I really sensed the Lord's protection as we continued to drive, surrounded by flames. All I could do was pray that God would save us. I was totally gripped with fear, a fear like I had never felt before.

Burnt cars on the road.

Chapter 4

Escaping The Fire

The whole time, our passenger was crying and panically saying, 'You are heading towards the pub!' In the blackness, you lose all sense of direction, and he had come from the direction of the pub, so he was trying to work out where we were and thought we were heading in the wrong direction, but no one knew what the right direction to travel was.

This whole time we were engulfed in a wall of fire, red everywhere. There were four cars blocking the road in front of us. They had just crashed into each other and exploded. I thought we would be stuck and unable to get away when suddenly it was as if the flames parted like the Red Sea, and we were clear of the flames.

I looked to my left, and there was a clear paddock that the fire had passed over. A light shone down onto the paddock as though the Lord was saying, 'Stop here.' Darren then asked,' Should we stop here?' I just said, 'Yes.'

I remember the eeriness of that moment; burnt-out cars in front of us, a car parked in the paddock next to the house, which I assumed was the owners, and a house still standing, even though the house next door to it had burnt to the ground.

The wind had stopped, and the fire had a weather pattern of its own; lightning was all around. It was as if we were in the eye of the storm. The car next to the house was indicating with their lights to us.

Fear again rose up on the inside of me as I realised we were in a car that had petrol in it and it was melting around us. We were effectively sitting in a bomb that could explode at any moment. Darren told us all to get down as low as we could. I looked behind me into the back seat and saw Samuel dripping in sweat. It was as if he had been in a swimming pool. I leant forward and prayed, 'Lord, if you're going to take us, make it quick and don't leave anyone.' I felt a real peace come over me, and at that moment, I was ready to die and be in the presence of my Lord and Savior.

When I opened my eyes, I couldn't believe it; instead of finding myself in heaven in the presence of my Lord, I was still in this random paddock.

Darren told us all, on the count of three, to simultaneously open the doors and get out of the car and run into the paddock. We were expecting the car to explode and kill us all, but miraculously it didn't; it just sat there. After a few minutes, Darren drove our car into the paddock.

I kept thinking, why are we here, and where are we? The wind picked up, and we were again engulfed in smoke. As we ran across the burnt paddock towards the house, cars drove in from both directions. The cars were full of people badly injured or badly burnt, not just families, but full of strangers that people had picked up. The stranger we had with us had burns to both arms and hands. My boys were able to access water from the house water tank, and I was able to get him to place his arms in a bucket that was nearby.

In the haste of leaving our house, I had left my phone behind. Jordan had his phone with him. I miraculously was able to call 000 standing in the middle of the paddock.

I didn't know exactly where I was but told the operator I needed an air ambulance immediately and that they could land in the paddock because it was clear. I told her Kinglake was gone and that we needed help, and there were thirty people with us. She kept telling me to calm down and that she would be the judge of whether we needed an ambulance or not. She asked me for an exact address, which I didn't know. All I knew was that we were in a paddock on the Kinglake-Whittlesea Road.

At the moment I was telling her this, the wind came up, blowing the smoke away, revealing that we were opposite Deviation Road, so I gave her this information. She kept asking me to clarify the address, saying, 'Kinglake? Is that Victoria?'

At that moment, I knew I wasn't talking to a local Victorian emergency operations unit and that they had no idea where Kinglake even was, so we were on our own. Jordan also got a call out to my brother Max to let him know we were okay and that we would be down to his place when we could. They were the only calls we were able to make from Jordan's phone because the fire had taken out all the mobile towers in Kinglake.

Back at the house, more cars were pulling in with injured people on board. Some had crushed ribs from being in car accidents trying to flee the fires. Others had chest pain and severe burns, and others said they were diabetics who had lost their medications in burnt-out vehicles. Many were telling harrowing tales of being separated from family, and they didn't know where their family members were or if they were safe. Some had escaped from the four vehicles that had exploded on the road, blocking our escape, and knew that their family members had died in those vehicles.

Being a Registered Nurse, I went into automatic nurse mode, assessing people's injuries and trying to do my best to help them. I knew I needed pain medication for the burns victims, so one of the men and I broke into the house to see what medications they had.

At first, all I found were herbal medications, and I remember thinking, 'Oh, not a natural remedy person; I need the strong stuff.' As we looked in a higher cupboard, I was relieved to find not only Panadol but Panadeine Forte as well. I needed all the help I could get.

Out of the darkness, a four-wheeler appeared. On it was David, the owner of the house. He was so glad to see us all and amazed that his house was still standing. He told us he had been with his parents on their farm and that they had all survived by getting into their dam. He had been in contact with his wife Jemima, telling her not to try and come home (she was at work downtown) and that their house was gone. So he was shocked not only to see his house standing but thirty random strangers sheltering there. He pointed me to where we could get drinks and food and told us to use anything we needed, and then he was gone.

For the next few hours, I tended to the injured, not knowing when we would get any help. The curtains caught on fire at the back of the house, and Jordan and Darren put them out, so we all had a safe place to shelter. I had put one of the burns patients inside the front door and spent the next couple of hours pouring water over his legs and feet that were badly burnt. All the time I was doing this, I felt guilty that I was ruining the carpet with the water, but I had to keep going.

During this time, Darren, Jordan and some other young men were making sure the house was safe from any further breakouts of fire by patrolling the perimeter of the property.

All night you could hear explosions of the transformers from the electricity grid nearby as well as gas bottles exploding from nearby properties. I remember the thought going through my mind that if one of these transformers hits you, you would be killed, so we better not stand out in the open.

Meeting Jemima and saying sorry for ruining their carpet with water.

Chapter 5

Leaving The Mountain

A few hours had passed, and I noticed our red Mitsubishi Magna leaving the paddock. I ran over to Jordan to find out what was happening, and he said that Dad and another man were going back into Kinglake to see what was happening.

When Darren returned, he told me that our house was gone and there was nothing left. The town was still very much on fire. He had driven to where the motorbike and cars had crashed, which we now know was opposite the broccoli farm.

He had checked the car that our stranger had said his wife was in, but there was no sign of her. Darren locked the Mitsubishi, and he and the other gentleman ran the rest of the way into town. Darren ran past the pub, down Glenburn Rd, towards our house and said he ran straight past our house because it was unrecognisable. There were burnt-out cars that had crashed on our road embankment. When he knew there was nothing left, he ran back to the car and came straight back to us.

I could see the despair on his face as he told me everything was gone. Because I was in automatic nursing mode and concentrating on my patients, the gravity of what he was saying didn't really sink in at the time.

During the night, Samuel was busy looking after a small boy who was with his grandparents. The Game Boy Samuel has rescued was an excellent distraction for both of them. When Darren returned, I will never forget the sight of him lying down in the corner with Samuel, looking completely defeated, and I thought, if you give up, what hope have we got. Darren had always been the strong one who knew what to do.

Finally, hours later, we saw a convoy of fire trucks and ambulances coming up the hill. A couple of paramedics assessed the injured, gave them pain relief, and said, 'We have to go; it is worse in Kinglake.'

I couldn't believe it. All I could say was, 'What, you are going to leave these people again when it's been hours, and they have already been put in jeopardy?' They assured me that they would return and get them on the way back, so I stood on the small front porch watching the ambulances and fire trucks heading toward the Kinglake township.

It felt like I was in the movie *Apocalypse*, and I was starring in it. It was such a surreal feeling. I thought to myself, 'How can it be worse in Kinglake?' but I didn't understand the enormity of the situation.

It was amazing that amongst the thirty people in that random place, we had a vet nurse, a forensic scientist and myself, a Registered Nurse. The ambulances and fire trucks did come back, and fire teams offered to escort anyone whose cars were mobile off the mountain in convoy.

Our passenger was the first to be evacuated because he could sit up in the passenger seat of a fire truck. I felt so relieved when he was being taken off the mountain to safety. Darren was keen to get the boys out to safety. I wouldn't agree to go until I knew all my patients were in an ambulance being taken to the hospital. When I waved the last one-off, I was happy to leave too.

We were now in a melted Mitsubishi, in the middle of the convoy of emergency vehicles, leaving our mountain and heading to safety. The severity of our situation became evident as we drove very slowly past burning houses, buildings and trees. Dead horses and other animals were lying lifeless on the sides of the road. Firefighters stopped at every burnt-out vehicle on the side of the road to check them. Huge tree branches on fire were still falling across the road, and emergency workers had to cut them with a chainsaw so the convoy could get through.

I felt so unsafe, with fear rising up within me once more. I said to Darren that maybe it would have been better to have stayed in the safety of the house. It took one and a half hours for the journey to Whittlesea, which would have usually taken twenty minutes.

Unbeknown to us, the Whittlesea Showgrounds had been set up as an emergency medical centre to assess patients before they were taken to the hospital. Due to the unsafe conditions, the emergency services had been waiting for hours to be able to come up the mountain.

As we approached the Showgrounds, the fire trucks ahead of us pulled over and waved us through. I could see the ambulances pulling into the Showgrounds as we drove by. Looking around the houses and the town, it was as if the world had stood still for us.

Our world was changed forever, but the rest of the city was the same. As we drove past the houses in Whittlesea in those early hours of the morning, lights were off as people slept, and street lights lit up roadways. Everything appeared calm and peaceful as we drove through the suburbs towards my brother's house, yet everything within me was shattered and in turmoil.

We eventually arrived at my brother's house in Saint Helena, where Max and his wife, Michelle, opened the door and hugged us and cried. We were four people standing at their door, covered in soot and smelling like we had come out of a bushfire. We were feeling totally defeated but knew that this was a place of safety and love.

The burnt-out shell of our Subaru.

What was left of our beautiful dining table.

What used to be Jordan's bedroom.

Chapter 6

Left With Nothing

Standing at my brother's front door, we only had the clothes on our back. Everything else had been destroyed. My brother took us in and proceeded to take the boys and me into the bathroom, where he washed our feet. I only had white shorts, a T-shirt and sandals on my feet, not great firefighting clothing and the boys were the same. I noticed that Samuel only had one shoe on.

At that moment, I realised that he had run across a burnt paddock with one bare foot, and he had no burn or injury to him. In the panic of getting into the car, only one of his shoes had been thrown in - another reminder of the Lord's faithfulness and protection over my family.

When I finally went to bed and tried to get some sleep, all I could see was the flames of the fire every time I closed my eyes. It was at that moment that I truly understood the gravity of our situation. I went into the toilet, and the emotions overtook me. I cried and cried, and I couldn't wait for the light of morning to come.

I asked my sister-in-law, Michelle, what time Target opened because we didn't have any clothes. We found ourselves in Target, getting the essentials that we needed. I was watching the boys trying on shoes, and it struck me that this reminded me of my trips to South Africa in 2005 and Zambia in 2008, on two separate short-term mission trips.

I found myself buying clothes for my family, who now had nothing, just like I had done in Africa for the AIDS orphans months before. I never imagined that my own family would be in a similar situation of having nothing.

In September 2005, I went to South Africa for a three-week short-term mission trip with a team from the church we belonged to, *New Horizons* in Whittlesea. They were a very mission-focused church that had partnered with an organisation called *Hands at Work* in South Africa, established by a married couple. They were white South Africans working with black South African communities and trained up volunteers from their own communities. These volunteers would go out and find those in need, and through *Hands at Work*, would then provide food, medical care, build houses, and establish schools and build kindergartens. *Hands at Work* met people's physical, emotional and spiritual needs.

Our team prepared for months what we needed to take and what role each of us would play, and we prayed together regularly. But, no amount of preparation could prepare me for what I saw as I arrived in Johannesburg and travelled by bus to White River.

The bus ride itself was terrifying as cars, trucks, and buses sped past. We were about an hour into our journey, and I had been sleeping. When I opened my eyes, I saw a town coming up in the distance, but it wasn't like a town I had ever seen before. I asked one of the other team members, who had been here before, what the town was in the distance, and she told me it was a shanty town. The houses were made of tin or scrap metal, and some were even made of cardboard. There were no roads, old car wrecks, dogs running around, people walking with bare feet, wearing worn-out clothes and children running around.

I noticed that there were armed guards at the gate and high fences with razor wire on the top, and these fences were separating this area from an area that contained houses like ours. This was nothing like I had ever experienced before, and I was told it was necessary because of a very high incidence of crime.

Sealed roads and electricity wires came across the top of the shanty town to provide electricity to this wealthy area. I was told the shanty town wouldn't have any electricity or running water. You had the poor living right next door to the rich. Tears ran down my cheeks as I realised that these were people who literally had nothing.

Due to the poverty of the local village nearby, it was known that foreigners came here to help and had money. I then knew I wasn't in a safe country like Australia.

The days following saw me going into the Masoi village with volunteer nurses. They would visit patients who had been referred by volunteers living in the community, and I was shocked to see the conditions these people lived in. The weather was scorching, and most houses were made out of corrugated iron sheeting, with dirt floors in most and just a bed or mat on the floor. Some had a portable gas cooker, but there was no running water, and people had to walk for quite a distance to collect water.

Most of the people we saw had AIDS, children were orphaned due to both parents dying of AIDS, and most were HIV positive.

These people couldn't afford medication, and one lady I remember, she would have been in her late twenties, was lying outside under a tree on a very thin mat. She was just skin and bones and could barely lift her head or arms and was close to death. There was no protection, no comfort or dignity, and all we could do was pray with her.

Another girl we visited, around seventeen years of age, was living alone in a corrugated iron shack with a dirt floor, a single bed, and she had a dirty blanket wrapped around her even though it was so stifling hot in there, I could hardly breathe. She too, had AIDS, and I was told that she was continually raped at night by local men. Another young girl we visited had syphilis, and the care workers had been trying to take her to the local medical centre for treatment, but her father wouldn't let them take her.

I was told that the village was controlled by the Witch Doctor, and he told the people not to trust the white man or their medicine. The people believed that AIDS was a lie from the white men, but even though they denied the existence of AIDS, the Witch Doctor told them that the cure for AIDS was to have sex with a virgin. So all these young girls were raped and contracted not only AIDS, but all other types of sexually transmitted diseases.

On hearing all these things, I became angry and saddened that this was going on in this day and age.

As I walked through the village, I noticed that we saw many older people, Grandmothers, grandfathers and children, but not many middle-aged people. On getting back to our accommodation, I asked Pastor Shane about it, and he said that people in our age bracket had died of AIDS, and only the elderly and the children were left. This was why the children were referred to as AIDS orphans, and some of these children were HIV positive. They were being raised by their grandparents, or older siblings were raising younger ones. In some households, the oldest child would only be eight or ten years old and responsible for raising their younger siblings.

Hundreds died every day; it was mind-blowing, and I asked others what the South African government was doing about it. As it was a black South African government, I was told that they just let them die because the problem was so big. I just couldn't grasp the vastness of this situation.

I also visited schools that had been set up by *Hands at Work*. These were set up for children that were orphaned and couldn't afford to go to school. It was amazing watching volunteer teachers teaching in buildings that had nothing, although they were fortunate if they had desks and chairs to sit on. Each child was full of joy and eager to learn, and the volunteers were also full of joy and loved what they did.

The little ones in the kindergartens that had been established and built by *Hands at Work* international volunteers like us enabled these little ones to have a safe place to come to. They would get a meal, which in most cases would be the only meal they would get for the day and play and learn.

One day I was at one of the kindergartens, and I saw a little boy being pushed over by another child. This little one, three years of age, was crying, and my motherly instinct kicked in. I picked him up and sat him on my knee to comfort him. He nestled in, and after a while, he became heavy as he relaxed, and when I looked down, he was fast asleep. One of the teachers came up to me and said that this was amazing, as he usually never went to strangers. I felt so privileged that I could give him motherly love when his mum was no longer around to give it to him.

Even though the people were so poor, they gave and shared freely what little they had. I felt love and acceptance, and there wasn't a moment that I felt afraid as I walked through the village. I knew God as with me, and all I wanted to do was share God's love with each and every person I encountered.

Whenever I went to visit someone, they always wanted me to pray with them. The needs seemed insurmountable. One day I was sharing how I felt so helpless. How was I helping in any way because the need was so great?

Another international volunteer shared this story with me; 'One day, a man was walking along a beach and saw a starfish washed up on the sand. He bent down, picked it up, and threw it back into the sea. As he walked a little further down the beach, he saw another starfish. He bent down again, picked it up and threw it back into the sea. As he looked, he noticed the beach was covered in starfish, so he bent down, picked another one up, threw it into the sea and said, "One more saved." One by one, he threw them back into the sea.'

I realised that the problem in South Africa was so large, like a beach covered in starfish, I just had to help one person at a time, and I wanted each person that I met to know the love of God that was in me and that someone cared.

In September 2008, I went with another team from the *New Horizons* church to Zambia. *Hands at Work* operate in many different African countries, and we ran a camp there for the most vulnerable children. Another team member and I went into town to buy brand new clothes and sandals with money that had been generously donated by people back home.

As each child received the clothes, they were so excited; there was so much joy and laughter as the children excitedly paraded in front of everyone to show off their new clothes. These were children with nothing but the joy and love in each one of them showed me they had everything.

Both these trips were preparing me for Black Saturday, the 7th of February 2009, where I would find myself homeless, losing everything I owned and treasured. My children and I found ourselves with nothing, being only able to draw on our faith and the love and protection of our Lord. Would we stand and praise the Lord like the Africans did when we had nothing?

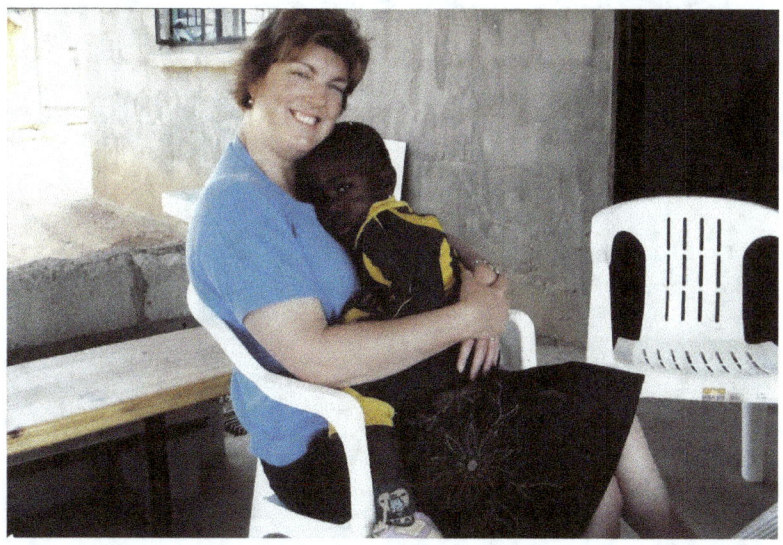

A moment of intimacy.

Spending time at the school.

At a camp in Zambia.

A grandmother hand rendering the walls of the school.

Chapter 7

Feeling The Love

It wasn't easy coping with life after the Saturday that changed our lives forever.

Our lives as we knew it had ended, and everyone else's just went on as normal as if nothing had happened. I could hear people having normal conversations around me, and I felt like an alien in an alien land. I felt such a sense of pain and aloneness at that moment.

We had driven our melted Mitsubishi Magna to the shopping centre, and as we were walking back towards the entrance, I noticed people would look and then stop to take a second look. This reinforced to me that it was hard for people to comprehend what we had been through. People could acknowledge the event and be caring, but they could never really understand unless they had gone through the fire. This left me with feelings of aloneness and, at times, anger when I thought people were going on living their lives and had forgotten or didn't really care about our situation. But, of course, it was reasonable that they got on with their lives; it was just sometimes difficult to cope with.

When we arrived back at Max and Michelle's, my Mum and Dad had arrived. They had managed to drive from Korumburra, and my uncle and aunty were there as well. Mum and Dad just held us. I told them what I had prayed in the car when we had stopped in the paddock, 'Lord, if you are going to take us, make it quick and don't leave anyone.' Mum replied, 'That wasn't what we were praying.'

Darren finally was able to speak to his parents in New Zealand. I'll never forget the sight of him crying and saying to his dad, 'I don't know what I'm going to do; there is nothing left.' The phone was continually ringing with people wanting to find out how we were and if we were all safe.

Pastor Shane and Millie, from the *New Horizons Church* in Whittlesea, which we were members of, turned up that evening with four suitcases full of clothes for each of us. Pastor Shane said that the church building was full of donated items. The ladies of the church had put together clothes that they thought would fit us and that we would like.

This was another one of God's wonderful provisions and a reminder of his love and care for every detail of our lives. I was so thankful for everyone's love towards us and for supporting us in our time of need. I was so overcome with gratitude for the love shown towards us from our family, friends and even people we didn't know.

I was so overwhelmed as I hadn't expected any help at all. We had spent the last few hundred dollars in our bank account at Target. Another very close friend arrived with clothes as well for the boys. He had toothbrushes, toothpaste, hairbrushes, and things I never thought about needing.

Through all of this, Pastor Shane had asked if we knew anything regarding another one of the church families because they hadn't heard from them or any news about them. It was at that moment that the thought dawned on me that they might not have made it, but I pushed the thought away as quickly as it had come.

A few days later, the news came that the entire family had perished. I questioned why we had survived, and they hadn't? There was an overwhelming feeling of guilt and immense grief when I thought about them. For my own survival, I tried not to think about those that had perished. One hundred and seventy-three lives were lost throughout Victoria in the Black Saturday bushfires, and many areas have memorials to remember and honour those lost.

During this time, unbeknown to me, my beautiful friend in Samoa had been praying Psalm 91 over our lives, while running on a treadmill. She had no idea what was happening to us but just had the Lord prompt her to pray and recite this Psalm for us.

She later saw footage on the news of the fires and immediately knew why she had been prompted to pray at that exact moment in time. God is so good. He places people in our lives who can stand with us and know His voice so well that they obey immediately.

She couldn't contact us, so she got her mum in Port Macquarie to ring around and find out what was happening with us. It took a couple of days, and her mum spoke to me on the phone and was able to let my friend and her husband know we were alive and well.

Chapter 8

Australia's Generosity

On the Sunday night, the night after the fires, Pastor Shane told us we needed to come to Whittlesea. A relief centre had been set up, and we needed to register our names with the Red Cross. As we parked our car, I couldn't believe what I was seeing. There were people everywhere; the Red Cross, Centrelink, Telstra and Vic Roads were all set up to assist.

As I walked through, I thought, this must be what a refugee centre is like. Then it suddenly dawned on me,

I was a refugee, coming for help because I now had nothing.

We walked into the centre, and suddenly people were approaching us, asking 'What is your name? Where are you from? Did you lose your house?' Others directed us to where there were donations of clothes and personal items.

I felt numb. I just wanted to get out of there. Suddenly people I knew were calling out my name; total looks of panic and despair on their faces. They, too, had been affected by the fires. They were so relieved to see familiar faces but then told us they couldn't find members of their family.

I could physically feel the tangible panic in the air as people were trying to locate family and friends. I felt very sad and upset for them but thankful that my family had remained together and all of us were safe. A board had been set up, and messages were put on it of people who were missing and unaccounted for. The atmosphere was full of panic and anxiety, mixed with relief when you saw someone you knew was safe.

We were directed outside, where restaurants had been set up, and people were cooking food for everyone. Again, the generosity of people was amazing. As we sat as a family, we were approached by the Today Show. They were interviewing the kids, and Jordan spoke with them. I appreciated how much he had grown up in just one day. He was only 17 years old but, due to this circumstance, had to become a man.

The next morning my uncle and aunty, who were in Queensland on holiday, saw the interview, which showed them that we were safe. So, the media also had a part to play in helping people find one another.

Pastor Shane then asked us to come back to the church to see the generous donations of people. The church hall, which used to be full of rows of chairs, now had trestle tables filling the room, piled high with clothes and linen, all donated by people not even 24 hours after the fire had destroyed our lives. It was hard to take in. Volunteers were sorting clothes that had been donated into men's, women's and children, sorting into sizes so people could easily find what would fit them.

As we were in the church hall, Jordan suddenly burst through the door with a reporter from the *Marie Claire* magazine in toe. He sat himself down in the corner and began telling our story. He was pointing over to Darren, Samuel and me. Next minute we found ourselves also being interviewed.

It was just amazing how Australia was rallying together to help. I had no idea that I had just lived through the worst disaster in Australian history at the time. We had no comprehension of how many homes had been lost, how many lives were lost, and people injured. At that moment, it was so special understanding and seeing the best in people and how loved we were by friends, family, the church family and the wider communities. We didn't know it then, but even people from other Australian states and even other countries were helping in whatever way they could.

Even people we didn't personally know wanted our bank details so they could give money to us directly to help us as a family. Churches, councils, and community groups worked together to help distribute donations and provide counselling; it was just amazing.

The Whittlesea Relief Centre was operational for weeks. Volunteers, all donating their time, were all so happy to sit with you and listen if you wanted to talk. Donations of food, clothes, shoes, and all sorts of goods, including TVs, fridges, furniture, and toys, continued to come in from the Australian community. There were even trucks full of goods coming from Queensland, even though they had just experienced floods.

People's generosity even extended to providing us with a house to live in. The assistant pastor of New Horizons church, who was also a volunteer in the CFA and another member of the CFA, had asked the assistant pastor if he knew of a family who needed a house to live in. They had one that was available, and they wanted to help, so that's how we got a house in nearby Whittlesea to live in.

One day I was at the relief centre with an aunty of mine, and she was encouraging me to take food items that had been donated. It was so overwhelming that all I took was a box of Weetbix breakfast cereal. That is what I thought we needed for the week, as I felt that others needed more. That was my thought pattern.

In the end, she had to take control because I wasn't comprehending that we were in need as much as everyone else. I was always the giver and found it so hard to receive charity from others. Looking back over this time, I remembered thinking, if you're going to go through a natural disaster, let it be in Australia. The Australian people came together to help in the darkest times. This wasn't just happening in Whittlesea; it was happening all over the State, at relief centres in Hurstbridge, Yea and Diamond Valley, just to name a few.

God had perfect connections to help us. Pastors from a church in Ringwood, came up to Whittlesea and spoke with Pastor Shane and his wife, Millie about how they could help. I had studied bible college through their church, and they were unaware that we had been affected by the fires.

While speaking with Shane and Millie, our name came up as one of the church families affected. They sponsored us financially, buying a computer that was lost in the fire so Darren could start his business again. Also covering many other financial needs, we had in the rebuilding process. God helped us by bringing us the people who assisted us in getting us back on our feet.

I received messages on Facebook from friends I had made in Africa, saying that we could come and live with them. These were people who were so poor and had nothing themselves, offering what little they had to us. That enforced God's love in action to me.

My colleagues at the Austin Hospital contacted me and asked if we could come into the ward on the Wednesday. When we arrived, we were overwhelmed by the love and support, not only from the nurses but also from the patients and their families. As I walked into the 6 West Ward, there was a great big sign that said, 'Please help Bron and her family'. I was taken to the Nurse Unit Manager's Office, where she handed me an envelope that contained money people had generously donated.

Unbeknown to me, the Today Show had come in to do a story on patients and staff that had been affected by the bushfires. They had asked the Nurse Unit Manager if they could contact me, and if I agreed, we would be interviewed.

The TV crew interviewed both of us at my brother's home late that afternoon. I found out later that because of that interview, more people were contacting the Ward wanting to donate money to help us. One of my nursing colleagues was sizing me up because Intimo was donating brand new bras for those affected.

We also received a phone call from Holden, who offered to loan us a new car for one year, which we accepted gratefully as both of our cars had now been written off by the insurance company.

Holden, and other car companies, donated many cars for people to drive for a year who had lost cars in the fires. Telstra replaced phones, and many companies offered assistance wherever they could.

One Sunday morning, I was at church, and one of my closest friends came across to me and placed something in my hands as I was praying. When I opened up my hand, there was a diamond ring in it. She knew how much losing my rings meant to me, and she gifted this ring to me. My beautiful Grandma Ellis also gifted me one of her rings.

This showed me that the Lord, through the love of family and friends and the wider community, is interested in every detail of our lives, continually showing His great love, care and faithfulness in our lives.

Chapter 9

Sifting Through The Rubble

The Thursday following Black Saturday was the first time residents were allowed to go back up the mountain. Police checked arm bands that indicated we were residents. As we drove, getting closer to our property, I had the strangest feeling of hope; that it had all been a dream and that my house would still be standing. Even though Darren had told me on the Saturday night that there was nothing left, I still held onto a glimmer of hope.

So, it was a feeling of absolute devastation when I saw the rubble that was once my home. It was the first house we had purchased, and I had raised my boys here. There were no words to describe the sense of loss and grief.

The area looked like a moonscape; black chard ground and burnt trees. Houses around us looked like ours, unrecognisable and totally destroyed. The *Marie Claire* magazine photographer who had been with the reporter who interviewed Jordan at the church on the previous Monday night, asked if he could come up with us. I told him that it would be okay, but I didn't know then what to expect when I arrived at the property and how I would react. He agreed that if we asked him to stop taking photos, he would.

When we got out of the car, I immediately could smell the pungent odour in the air. Darren's Subaru was a burnt-out shell in what used to be our carport. Amazingly our trailer that was right next to the Subaru wasn't burnt and only had a blown-out tyre. This left me completely bewildered as to how indiscriminate the fire had been. Our house and car were totally destroyed, yet our trailer right beside our car had only minor damage.

One of Jordan's closest friends met us at our property. I'll never forget the sight of the boys sifting through the rubble of what used to be their rooms. Steel frame beds still stood, twisted and burnt. They began sifting through the rubble to see what they could find.

Sifting Through The Rubble

Darren and I went to where our bedroom had been and began sifting carefully through the rubble. I was looking for my engagement and eternity rings as I wasn't wearing them on the Saturday because it was so hot, and we were home.

We had gone to a hardware store in Whittlesea before we drove up and brought a sift for that exact job. We found all sorts of things, burnt, broken cups, and garden ornaments. I found various pieces of burnt jewellery, including my eternity ring with the diamonds still intact, but no sign of my engagement ring that I kept right next to it. Every piece found was a treasure to me, and all were placed in a bag or boxes. These were all remnants of our life, twenty years of memories.

Darren found the engine frame from what remained of his Buel motorcycle. We had a beautiful Blue Gum dining table with steel dining chairs, and the chairs still stood around the dining table that was now just a pile of ash. Twisted metal was everywhere. The photographer was so helpful; he even helped us sift through the rubble. As I look back now, I was grateful he was with us to document that day with the photos he took.

I needed to use the toilet and suddenly realised I didn't have one. I walked up to the main town, which was only 500 meters away. It was so strange. I felt like I was in another world; not only was our home reduced to a barred moonscape, but only 500 meters away, the township had also been transformed and was taken over by the army.

However, a few doors up from our property on the other side of the road, a neighbour's house had been totally spared. The family were sitting in their garage laughing and talking like they had been on the Saturday afternoon before the fires. I felt extremely angry walking past their house, questioning why their house had been spared by the fire and mine hadn't. It wasn't the most gracious emotion, but I couldn't help feeling this way.

To get to the toilet block, I had to walk through army tents that had been set up. I was in a total daze, not comprehending what had happened. A voice called out to me, and one of Samuel's friends came running up to me, asking me where Samuel was and excitedly telling me that a couple of the Australian cricket team players were coming up to play cricket with the kids. I was overwhelmed by the extraordinary generosity and display of love from the Australian people.

I was happy we had the photographer with us because he took photos of Samuel with one of the cricket stars. The player even gave Samuel the bat that they had been playing with and signed it for him. It captured a moment of joy for him in such devastating circumstances.

While I was standing with Samuel on the property, I heard someone calling out to me, asking if he could come up and talk with us about what had happened. He was a reporter from Sky News. I wasn't aware that a busload of reporters had come up who had been instructed not to approach anyone. Obviously, that wasn't going to stop him.

He came barreling up, cameras in our faces and asking us our story. At the time, I thought he was very rude and insensitive and didn't really care about us; he only wanted a story. I found out later that many people had seen that footage of Samuel and me on Sky News, and many had donated money to the bushfire appeal because of it. Again, God uses all sorts of methods for His purpose.

On the Wednesday following Black Saturday, I was watching the Today Show at Max's, and a story came on the TV of a couple that had been reunited in the Emergency Department of the Alfred Hospital. They had been separated while escaping the flames, and both feared that the other had perished in the fire.

I was pleasantly surprised to see the man we had rescued on the side of the road and his wife. I had been so worried about her since we were unable to help her due to the ferocity of the fire. I wouldn't have been able to forgive myself if she had perished. I was so happy and grateful to the Lord for his saving grace, so I got straight onto the phone to the Alfred Hospital and asked if I could speak to them. They put me through, and I spoke with our passenger's wife, and I told her how worried I had been about her, and I was so glad she was alive.

Ours was a story of hope in a hopeless situation and glimmers of hope, like finding my eternity ring and other jewellery in the rubble. God really showed me that he cared about every area of our lives and that He still remained faithful, watching over us and providing for us.

Months after the event, Darren asked me what I missed the most? He knew what my answer would be because every day, I would look at my fingers that no longer had my engagement ring on them.

Days after this conversation, we were shopping at Greensborough, and I found Darren looking in the window of a jewellery store. He told me to take a look, and to my astonishment, there was an engagement ring very similar to the one I had lost in the fire.

I hesitantly asked if I could try it on, my hands were shaking, and tears were flowing down my face as I explained to the shop assistant how precious and amazing it was to find this ring. More amazing was that not only was it so close in style, but it had a bigger diamond than my original ring. She then informed us that it was on special, and of course, Darren brought it for me. Even when I wear it today, I am so amazed at the goodness of God and how he cares for every detail of our lives.

I loved seeing the boys being gifted with toys and items, replacing the ones that had been destroyed. Jordan received an electric guitar and amplifier from Alan's music. This had been arranged by Plenty Valley College's music department as he was studying music in VCE. His year 12 friends took up donations of money and brought him an acoustic guitar to replace the one he had lost so he could continue his music. The love and generosity shown to my boys was wonderful.

Darren was a part of the local model flyers club, and members who had also gone through the fires arranged for other clubs to donate model planes so Darren could still continue his hobby.

One activity we always enjoyed as a family was bike riding together. Our friend, who had also gone through the fires, arrived at the house that we were renting in Kinglake with push bikes that had been donated. The generosity of people and friends who themselves were suffering, to think of us was absolutely amazing and humbling.

It took me around a year to be able to finally hand my eternity ring to a jeweller to repair. It had been in a plastic bag with all the burnt jewellery that I had managed to find in the rubble. I had it repaired and could once again wear it on my ring finger, perfectly matched with my wedding and new engagement ring. When I put it on, I couldn't stop admiring my rings.

At around the same time, I met up with a local jeweller and handed her all my burnt jewellery. She melted all my silver jewellery down and made me such a special necklace, creating something I could once again wear. She also introduced me to another jeweller on the mountain that worked with gold and diamonds.

He melted down the gold, and we designed a ring that incorporated other diamonds that we had saved from the fire. Again God showed me that he cared about the smallest details of our lives; that I could trust him with everything, and that he was continually with us and would never forsake us.

Trying to find my rings.

Sifting through Jordan's room.

Samuel comforted by Macca the horse.

Chapter 10

Five House Moves

I have heard it said that moving house is one of the most stressful things in your life. Well, try moving five times in a total of eighteen months.

We found our first move straight after the fire to the safety of my brother Max's house in Saint Helena. This came with feelings of fear, sadness and complete loss. We arrived on his doorstep with only the clothes on our backs. There must have been a big adjustment period for them because my brother and sister-in-law now had another four people living under their roof. Because of our circumstances, people were coming and going from their homes, dropping things off to us and visiting us, and the media came in and filmed our story. Phones were also continually ringing with friends trying to check on how we were.

A few days into our stay, Michelle had to tell me that I needed to stop taking all these calls because I wasn't eating properly. It was great having her speak up for me at times. Max and Michelle continued to work as well as deal with the upheaval of us in their lives. I so appreciated the love and safety that they gave us.

They had had their own trials leading up to this time, as Michelle had had trouble conceiving a child. They had been trying for years. A month before Black Saturday, I had felt the Lord say to me that I needed to pray into this situation they were having. We were all in church one Sunday morning, and I just came alongside Michelle and prayed that whatever it was that was stopping her from conceiving that the Lord would heal her and that she would be able to have a child. Because of events now happening, I didn't give it another thought. God's love for us is so good in the midst of our darkness. Michelle became pregnant, and their baby son Lucas was born in November 2009. He was a gift of hope and joy in the midst of pain.

Even in this safe place, I still longed to go home. The Lord knew that we needed to be living as a family in our own house. This is where the second house move happened. One of the CFA volunteers from the Whittlesea CFA had asked the assistant pastor at the New Horizons Church if he knew of someone who needed a house to live in. Her partner was living with her, and he had a house in Whittlesea that was for sale, with some furniture. He wanted to help the bushfire victims by allowing a family to live there. Before I knew what was happening, we were given this house, and we were moving what little possessions we had in - another amazing provision from our God.

There was a sense of anxiety and insecurity about leaving Max and Michelle's but knowing that our family needed to be a family living on our own as we continued to rebuild our lives one day at a time, made the decision an easy one. I was a step closer to moving back to the mountain – Every day, looking and longing to go home.

Even though this house had been a wonderful provision, my heart still was with my home in Kinglake. It's hard to describe that feeling and longing for home. Whittlesea wasn't my home. It was just a place to live for a time. Kinglake was our community, and I guess I didn't want the events of the fire that we had no control over, to force us to leave our community, and this is what drove our decision to eventually rebuild on our original property.

Everyday we were confronted with the site of dump trucks full of the remains of people's homes going to the tip. It was a place people could come to talk and pray together. We were so grateful for this couple's generosity; they allowed us to live there rent-free.

This house had been for sale for over a year, and a few weeks later, after we moved in, it sold. An older couple who had lost their home in the fires in Kinglake had brought it as they couldn't face rebuilding and moving back to Kinglake. Feelings of fear, panic and insecurity rose up within me as I realized we would have to find somewhere else to live. God again came through on our behalf.

Close friends of ours were getting married, and they offered us their home in Craigieburn to rent. I felt so unsettled about living in Craigieburn; it was further from Kinglake and my work at the Austin Hospital. It was an area I didn't know. I felt terrible that I was even questioning if this was the right move because we had nowhere else to go. I remember praying and saying to the Lord that if this was the provision He was giving, then I was thankful for it.

As I was praying, another friend called and said that she was speaking with a couple who hadn't lost their house in the Kinglake fires, and they were going to go around Australia, and they wanted to help bushfire victims who needed a home to rent for nine months. My friend mentioned us straight away. God knows every desire of our hearts. He knew I wanted to be back home on the mountain. This house was within walking distance to our property in, what we called, the new estate.

So, after two months of living in Whittlesea, we found ourselves packing up our belongings again and moving to our new home in Kinglake. Neighbours had donated furniture, and the owners had left some of their furniture in place for us to use. Beds had been donated, but I wanted the boys to have new beds, which we brought and had delivered. This house was perfect for us. It was large, with an office area already set up for Darren to work from. Jordan was studying year 12, so there was a large rumpus room that we gave him, so he had his own room and an area he could study and relax that could be closed from the rest of the house.

I just had an overwhelming feeling of relief as I was able to live back on the mountain. This was our community; this was our home. Neighbours and friends would again come over, and we could just talk, cry and pray together. Walking to the shops, I would meet people I knew, and we would just hug, cry and talk in the middle of the supermarket and the street. It was a time of connection and healing.

The owners of the house ended up coming back earlier than planned. The amazing thing was that they left us living in the house while they lived in their caravan in a large shed on the property; such amazing generosity. They ended up putting the house up for sale, and it sold in the nine months that we lived there.

Our new house that was being built by Kentucky Napier was not going to be ready when we needed to be out of the rented house. Again, I was overcome with feelings of anxiety and fear. Where were we going to live? We couldn't go back to Max and Michelle's because they had a new baby. I frantically went up to see if there was something in the Village that had been set up for temporary accommodation, only to be told they were full.

Darren remembered he had met up with an old client in Kinglake West months earlier. She had told him that she had managed to save both houses on her property on National Park road. She had given him her contact details if ever we needed anything, so we contacted her, and that's how we found ourselves moving for the fourth time to her house in Kinglake West.

We moved into what we affectionately called the Brown house on Liz's property. This was a one-bedroom cottage, again fully furnished. Liz lived in the other house on the property known as the White House. She had the most wonderful horse called Macca, and he became a great source of healing. You would be either lying on the bed or sitting in the lounge area, and he would come up to the window and, if it was open, pop his head in. Again, I felt safe here. New friendships were formed, and eternal bonds were made.

Our fifth house move would see us finally back to our new house on our block.

At the Brown house.

Samuel holding Lucas.

Chapter 11

Our House Arrival

One day, I had walked around to our property from the rented house and just sat down in the dirt, looking over at the footings for our new house and wondering if we had done the right thing in rebuilding.

Darren, at the time, considered the possibility of buying the Whittlesea house we were living in, but the boys and I just wanted to come back home.

Kinglake was our home, and the boys had been born here. Our family was very involved in the community, from the boys going to Kindergarten and primary school. They were involved with AusKick and basketball and had very established friendships in Kinglake. When we were living in Whittlesea, we had a discussion as a family about coming back to Kinglake, and the boys both said that they definitely wanted to come back because they were born there.

I didn't want the fire to force me away from my home; if I was going to move away, I wanted it on my terms.

It would have been much easier to have brought an established house and not have gone through the heartache of rebuilding on our block. Obstacles were put in the way everywhere we turned. We would be told one thing and then be told a couple of months later that new rules had come in and we had to change plans again.

We had a lot to think about because we were insured for the house but found out our insurance didn't cover contents or things like fences, water pumps, or replacement of the septic system, which we only found out as we started the rebuilding process. We were very underinsured, so as you can imagine, we have made sure we have adequate insurance now.

It was such a stressful and frustrating process, but through it all, the desire to come home was so strong.

Over the first few months, we had looked at different styles of houses. We had to meet a BAL29 rating which meant the house had to meet a specific design, and we had to take out a larger loan than we had initially taken out twenty years earlier.

After the fires, the government brought in a new BAL rating system which meant any new houses built in the area had to meet specific specifications, Bush Fire Attack Levels (BAL). Properties were assessed and given a rating depending on their location and the level of potential fire threat. The higher the number more fire-prone the property was.

Some properties, including some of our friends, were so high in the BAL rating that they were unable to build back on their properties and had to sell them to the government and buy or build a house elsewhere. Our property had a relatively high rating, so we needed to have specific features built. We had to have double glazed windows a specific height from the floor, Merbau decking, and it had to be built with a fire-resistant cladding or brick. It also had to have stainless steel meshing on the windows and on the security doors. All these specific requirements put up the cost of rebuilding.

We eventually decided on a transportable home. It was built by Kentucky Napier, in Bayswater in their factory and then would be delivered in sections and reconstructed onto our block. We decided to do this because Kinglake weather can be really wet in winter, and the thought was that if the house wasn't built on the block, it would be a much quicker process. Another advantage was that these houses were built to meet the BAL requirements.

The first thing built on our block was a shed and carport. I never thought I would say it, but I was very excited as we began building the shed. Something concrete was going up on our block after it had stood empty for around nine months. Finally, the day had arrived that our new house was being delivered - twelve months after Black Saturday.

It was delivered in the week of the first anniversary of Black Saturday, February 2010. We were still living in the rented house around the corner from our block. I received the call to say that the trucks would be bringing up our house and would be parking in the pub's car park. I excitedly ran around to the pub and stood waiting for the first truck to arrive with the part of our house and the second truck with another section. It looked like a doll's house, one part had the kitchen exposed, the other part had the bathroom and toilet exposed, and there was no roof.

The third truck arrived with the top of the house in two parts. 'Neighbours were gathering around to see and asking, 'Is this your house?. It was so exciting. The clouds were gathering, and I was worried it was going to rain and cause damage to the internal structures, so I quickly called up Kentucky Napier to see if they were coming up to place protective tarps over it.

When I was told that the house would stay in the car park overnight, the thought occurred to me that someone would use the toilet before I had a chance to use it, but of course, there was no plumbing.

The next morning all four of us excitedly arrived on our block to watch the house delivery. The large crane was already in position, and the first part of the house was coming down the back track. There were lots of whistling and hand gestures by the workers as the house was reassembled; each piece was placed in the exact position. At that moment, all the hardships and obstacles of rebuilding were all worthwhile. Of course, the house wasn't complete and ready to move in; it would be another three months before we would get the key.

There was still a massive amount of work to be completed. The staircase needed to be put in, plastering, flooring, plumbing, and electrical work needed to be completed, and the front and back verandahs were still to be built. My Dad came to live with us in the one-bedroom cottage. He had come to help us paint the inside. So now there were five of us living in the Brown house. Every paint stroke I made helped me to connect with the new house. Family and friends all came to help with the painting; their way of showing us how much they loved us and wanted to help in any way they could.

The furniture arrived on the Friday before Mother's Day, and we finally moved in on Mother's Day, May 2010.

We were finally home, but it didn't feel like home. Even though it sat in the exact position of the old house, it felt strange and different. Once I stopped working on the house, I became very depressed and cried a lot. I walked around the new house, amongst all the brand new furniture. Everything from the past was gone, so nothing from the old house was in this new one. I felt like I was living in a display home. This wasn't my home or my furniture. I didn't have any of the treasures that I had collected over the past 20 years, all of which had a story behind them. I felt guilty that I felt this way. I should have felt happy and grateful, but the truth was, I didn't.

As I looked out into the yard, there was nothing familiar, everything had been dug up for plumbing to go in and the new septic system installed. The only thing that was the same was the concrete water tank. We would have to begin the daunting task of beginning again with all the landscaping - so much work to be done.

Our original property had a very established garden which Darren and I had meticulously built over the past 20 years. But I found myself looking at a completely blank canvas wondering where to start. We got landscapers to at least build retaining walls and garden beds. Then over time, we were able to begin planting new trees and shrubs. I spent time researching the best fire-resistant plants to put in. It took years, but as I look out into the garden now, it looks well established, so different from the moonscape that followed after the fire.

I felt healing was happening with every hole I dug and every plant I put in, but it took me many years, probably around five years, before this new house became my home.

The first thing we rebuilt was our shed.

Half of our house being delivered.

The house starts to take shape.

Almost There.

At the end of the day of construction.

Our new home starts to take shape

Chapter 12

Special Bonds Formed

Living back on the mountain, I would go to the supermarket for something and be standing in the middle of an aisle and crying with someone I knew. We listened to each other and comforted one another. Even though this was hard, I felt that connecting with others was a major part of my healing process. People who had gone through the fire experience understood me. Even though people who hadn't gone through this experience tried to help by listening to me when I was down, they couldn't understand the depth of my grief.

I felt very alone at times. Even within the community, there were so many different experiences. Some lost everything they owned; others lost everything as well as their family and friends. Others still had their houses that had been saved. Those people voiced feelings of guilt that their houses were standing and I had lost mine.

I remember sitting in a friend's kitchen and saying how I loved that their house was still here because how else would I be able to come and sit and have a coffee if it was also gone. I loved the fact that their house and furniture were the same as before the fires. It was something comforting and familiar in a time when nothing was familiar to me.

Pastor Shane came up one day while we were still living at the rental house and told us that he had put our family forward for a trip to New Zealand.

The New Zealand people had been so touched by the devastation that had happened that money was raised by a radio station, MoreFM, in Rotorua on the North Island. Doctors, Pastors, and Social Workers had all been asked to nominate people who were badly affected so they could fly over to New Zealand for a much-needed holiday, all expenses paid. Another amazing act of kindness.

Ten people were selected, including Darren, Samuel and me. Jordan also was selected but opted not to come because he went to New Zealand with his school just after the fires. That was also a wonderful provision from God because, at the time, we didn't know how we were going to pay for his trip and a very dear friend who I had grown up with wanted to pay for him to go. Darren is a New Zealander, and his parents live in Havelock North on the North Island, so it was a chance for us to catch up with them as well.

The day came when we arrived at the airport. We were unsure who else was coming and only knew there would be a small group of us. As we looked around, we saw an elderly couple who looked lost, and I said to Darren, 'I think they will be in our group,' and yes, they were.

There was another middle-aged lady with her daughter, a lady on her own, who we later found out was alone because her husband couldn't get a replacement passport in time. He had gone to the airport in the hope that an emergency one would be issued so he could fly. Unfortunately, that didn't happen, so now our group would be nine. At that time, we didn't see the ninth person on the trip.

As we were waiting to check-in, there appeared to be a problem with my replacement passport, and they were debating whether I would be allowed to fly. When I received my replacement passport months earlier, it had only six months left before it expired. I became very anxious and tearful, but Darren, as always, was the voice of reason, saying it would be fine and not to worry.

I was eventually cleared to travel, and we had to make the mad dash to International departures to go through customs. When we finally arrived in

Auckland, we met the ninth person in our group. We were met and transported to Rotorua by bus. It was a great time to start to get to know those we were travelling with. We were all from different fire-affected communities.

The older couple was from Marysville, another lady was from Upper Plenty, a mother and daughter were from Clonbinane, and another lady was from Kinglake. She lived only a couple of kilometres from us, but we had never met. And, of course, Darren, Samuel and I were from Kinglake. Each of these people had different experiences in the fire, miraculous escapes similar to ours. Some had lost everything, and some had illnesses and injuries.

It was when we landed at Auckland airport that we finally met the ninth member of our group. She had been severely injured in the fires and required a wheelchair or crutches to get around. We fast became friends, and the whole group became like a family, bonded through tragic circumstances.

This trip enabled us to laugh together, cry together and experience new things. The most important was the healing that came through a common bond. I am so grateful I went on this trip meeting, not only what I refer to as my New Zealand family, but also those that looked after us so well on this five-day trip. Darren, Samuel and I hired a car from Rotorua and, at our own expense, drove down to Havelock North to spend a further five days with Darren's parents.

I had formed such a bond with our New Zealand family that I felt really sad when they got on the bus to drive back to Auckland to catch their flight home, and we weren't joining them.

Once the house had arrived, we wanted to get a puppy for Samuel to help with his recovery. I got onto the internet and researched what kind of dog we wanted. Darren was allergic to dog and cat fur, so we had to buy a breed that didn't shed hair. I wanted a small house dog.

I found a lady advertising Maltese Shih Tzu puppies for sale. I explained our situation to her and that we weren't in a position to take the puppy home until we had moved back to our rebuilt house. She met Samuel and me in the school carpark with the puppies in toe. She could have sold every one of them as the kids dragged their parents over to have a look. Samuel finally chose a male, which was the smallest of all the puppies, and he was going to name him Henry.

He begged and pleaded for us to take him home, then and there, but I explained it was unfair on the puppy to take him back to the Brown house and then move him to our new house in a couple of weeks. Reluctantly he agreed to leave him with the breeder, and we would pick him up after we moved.

The day arrived that all the new furniture that had been stored for us finally was being delivered. It was so exciting. Darren and I were at the house putting everything in place when the breeder phoned. I thought she was calling to make a time to pick Henry up, but she was very upset, and she told me that when she went to where the puppies were sleeping, she noticed something was wrong with Henry. By the time she had driven to the vet, he had died.

I was in shock and speechless. She was so upset because she knew our story and why we were getting Henry. I reassured her that these things happened and it wasn't her fault, and I quickly asked if there were any puppies left. She said they had all been sold, but she did have one left, a female and the only tri-colour like Henry. She had planned to keep her for breeding; however, she offered us this puppy if we wanted it. I didn't know how I was going to break the news about Henry to Samuel.

When Samuel arrived home from school, I told him about Henry, which of course, made him very sad; however, as soon as I mentioned that there was a girl puppy available, he was quick to say yes. That's how our Coco came into our family.

She hasn't just been great for helping Samuel heal but has been a very big part of my healing journey. I never understood the healing power of animals until I experienced it for myself. Samuel is always complaining now that Coco was brought for him but that she loves me more, and even as I'm writing, she is lying next to me. I never knew I could love a dog so much. The Lord uses so many different ways to bring healing and restoration into our lives.

During this unravelling time, I also became involved with an equine-assisted program called the *Matanya*

Effect. Horses were the teachers in this program, and I found out the healing power of working with horses as well. I had experienced it early on with Liz's horse Macca when we lived in the brown house. If I was feeling down, I would go outside and give this huge animal a cuddle and just cry. He had an amazing effect on me. I only realised the full effect when I took part in this horse program.

Samuel and Coco.

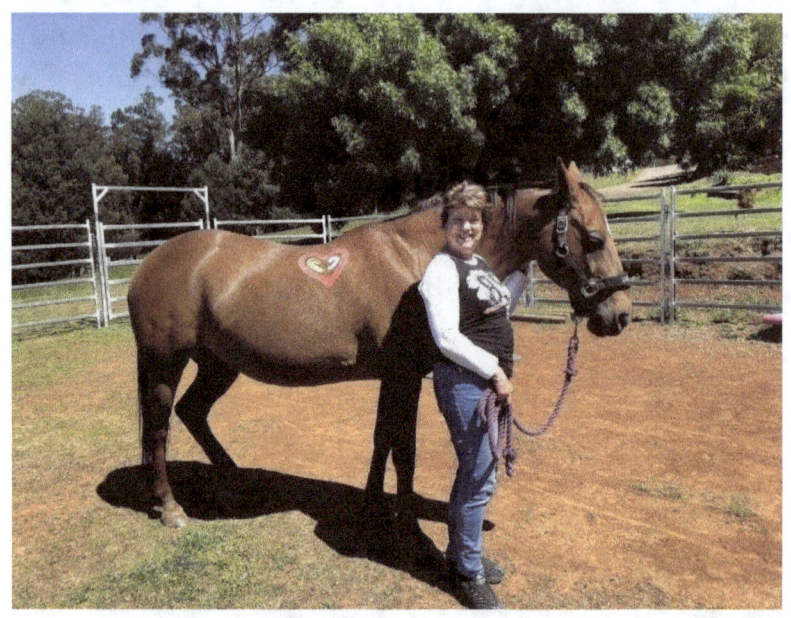

At Matanya with my horse teacher.

Chapter 13

A New Chapter

As I sit here contemplating twelve years on, I can see how far we have come as a family. This journey hasn't been easy.

I had many moments of grief and loss when thinking of friends who were no longer with us. Attending the memorial service for an entire family lost in the fires was heartbreaking as such a wonderful family was no longer with us. I was mourning the loss of one of our New Zealand family who had survived the initial fire, incredibly injured but looking forward to both of us rebuilding and continuing to build on this amazing bond and friendship.

I remember getting the most heartbreaking phone call while we were living in the Brown house to say that one of the members of our New Zealand family had passed away. It was total shock and disbelief and sadness knowing that she wasn't going to see her house rebuilt, and we couldn't continue our friendship. I questioned why? Realising I won't know the answer to these questions but allowing God's peace and comfort to come upon me. In amongst all these feelings, God continued to show himself faithful through the hard times.

I found myself totally unravelled as the years pressed on, even though I had accepted the 'New Normal'.

The ' New Normal' referred to our lives being totally changed by that fateful event. There was nothing left from our past way of life, and we had to build a new future. Even our community was different, with many people who had been affected, not returning. Old houses were gone, and new houses were built in their place. When I went up the street, I saw new faces and did not see some of the people I knew. Darren and I often would reach for something we had before the fire and then realise that it was gone. So we referred to these changes as the 'New Normal.'

This term is now being used to describe life after the COVID pandemic because our lives are no longer the same as they were before the pandemic. We felt this after Black Saturday.

In mid-2017, Jordan introduced us to a wonderful girl he had been communicating with. Taleisha was from

Gympie in Queensland. She had flown down for the weekend with her sister, who was engaged to Jordan's best friend. She had come down to Melbourne to finally meet Jordan in person.

From the minute I met her, I knew she was the one for Jordan. Of course, I stayed cool, calm and collected, and I invited her over for lunch so I could get to know her better. She ended up coming to Victoria to live, and she lived with us for nine months. Jordan asked her to marry him soon after her arrival, and they were engaged in September 2017.

Unbeknown to Darren and I, Jordan had wanted to get married on the Exton's property. This was the property we had escaped to on Black Saturday, and he asked Jemima and Dave if they could get married on their property. Of course, they said yes!

Jordan and Taleisha announced that was where they were getting married, and that both the ceremony and reception were going to be held there. At first, I didn't know how I felt about it. I had such vivid memories of that property of fire and destruction.

The closer the day came, the more anxious and apprehensive I became. I worried about how I was going to feel and react standing in the paddock again. People kept asking me how I felt about it, but I didn't have an answer.

All I knew was that this was what Jordan and Taleisha wanted, and I was excited for them about their wedding day and wanted it to be perfect for them.

Darren's Mum and sister arrived from New Zealand a few days before the wedding. Sharon (his sister) and I took a walk up to Frank Thompson reserve two days before the wedding. I was sharing my fears and anxiety with her, so we decided to go and stand in the paddock so I could feel any emotions that may come up.

I hadn't returned to the property since we had called in a few days after Black Saturday, and my heart was beating in my chest as I tried to see in my mind's eye, not flames, fear and destruction, but my son and his bride standing there so happy and in love.

It was March 9th 2018, and the morning of the wedding had arrived. Lots of running around, making sure everything was done and was perfect. We arrived where the ceremony was going to be, overlooking Melbourne. It was perfect weather, and Jordan and Samuel were standing there looking very handsome.

I had an overwhelming sense of joy and gratitude that we had survived, my boys were now young men, and I was about to have a new daughter-in-law, who I absolutely loved. So thankful to the Lord for his goodness and grace. He knew what the future held, and it was a great future.

I remember looking and walking towards the house on the property where we had sheltered with thirty strangers nine years before. I just stopped and prayed to thank the Lord that he had saved our lives that night so that this day could happen.

A happy and precious memory was formed that day on Jemima and Dave's property. A new chapter had begun in our lives. Black Saturday had been the start of a very different chapter in our lives, a chapter full of loss, grief and fear. March the 9th, 2018, was a new chapter of joy, hope, love and peace for all of us.

Jordan and Taleisha.

Our family.

Chapter 14

Fires Again Threaten Victoria And Australia

Eleven years on, the news channels were again reporting fires across Australia. New South Wales, ACT, South Australia, Victoria, Western Australia and Queensland. These fires were labelled as 'The Black Summer Bushfires (2019-2020)', and again images of frightened people, devastated land masses and destroyed homes were splashed across our television screens.

Feelings of anger welled up within me as I heard the same messages being said that we had listened to all those years ago. Initial cash payments of $1000 per adult and $400 per child were paid to help families start rebuilding their lives. To the public listening, this probably sounded like the government was doing something good, but over the past eleven years, the cost of living has gone up quite substantially, so I knew that this amount would not go far. However, I'm sure that, like us, they were grateful for any help.

Millions of dollars were raised by different organisations, and there was story after story of people not receiving the help they required. Politicians made statements that communities should be rebuilt in months. I knew it would take years for these families to rebuild their lives.

Feelings of despair rose within me. I felt the pain of these families that stood there in the ruins of their lives. I had been there eleven years earlier. Watching on brought back the hurt and absolute despair that I felt straight after the fires. You were in shock and constantly living under the flight and fight response that your body goes into in a traumatic situation. Your body runs on adrenalin to help you get through each day. As an observer, it sounded exactly as we had experienced eleven years earlier. Yes, we had received amazing support from family, friends and even people we had never met, but it still was a very hard and painful road to recovery, both financially and emotionally.

The pain never completely goes away, but you learn to adapt and move forward in your new normal. Talks again of a Royal Commission into the disaster, it felt like no one had learnt from Black Saturday.

A Royal Commission had been held after Black Saturday. After hearing many months of testimonies from people directly affected by the Black Saturday bush fires, sixty-seven recommendations were made by the Black Saturday Royal Commission. Some of these recommendations included new advice about preparing for bushfires, changing how houses were constructed and banning new homes in areas of high fire risk. So, why was there another one needed for these fires?

All I could do was pray for these families and communities that had been impacted. One practical way I felt I could help those struggling businesses was to buy their products online. Every little bit helps is what I have learnt from my own experience. Every time I looked at the television reports on the fires, I felt all those feelings of fear, hopelessness, and anxiety well up within me once more.

I really had to lean into the Lord so that I didn't take on more than I could bear. I was not taking on other people's trauma and experiences. I had to distance myself from this situation. I felt guilty at first, like I wasn't caring for these people and their situation. I felt the Lord say I had to protect myself from being traumatised by an event that wasn't happening to me.

I found myself reaching out for help from my psychologist, family and friends, who were such a great source of strength and comfort. I am so grateful for these people God has put in my life.

As I watched people, on television, in their burnt-out homes, sifting through the ruins, I prayed that the Lord would give them comfort and strength, just as He had done for my family and me. I knew it was going to be a long road ahead of recovery. Little did we know at the time, that all of Australia was going to be under threat, not from a natural disaster such as bushfires or floods, it was going to be from a pandemic of unprecedented proportions. This medical emergency was not just threatening Australia, but threatening the whole world.

Again, as I cried out to the Lord, I had a sense of His peace and protection. My heart cried out to Him for those that had gone through the fires, that they would find His peace, comfort, and strength in the midst of chaos.

Chapter 15

Corona Virus (COVID 19) Pandemic

We have found ourselves in the grip of this virus since March 2020, and a year later, we were still facing uncertainty, not knowing what would happen tomorrow, just like it was for us after the fires. There was uncertainty, fear and anxiety, and people's way of life was turned upside down with rules and regulations placed upon our lives by others that we couldn't control. This pandemic was worldwide, and no country was untouched; economies were crippled, and health systems placed under pressure. Millions were infected and dying all over the world, and leaders being put under the microscope. Even the United Kingdom Prime Minister was infected by the virus; no one was immune.

My thoughts turned to those still trying to recover from the recent bushfires, and I realised that they had been forgotten because a more pressing threat was developing. At this time, I have really been praying and seeking God's hand in this situation. As I sat in my home under stage 3 lockdown in rural Victoria, I was so grateful that I had this wonderful home to live in. I had food on the table, a loving family to care for. Daily I counted my blessings and thanked the Lord for all His provisions.

Just before this pandemic began, I was begging Darren for another dog. My friend Sally's Cavoodle had a litter of puppies in early December 2019, and both of us had been working on Darren to allow me to get one of the puppies, but his answer was continually, 'No. I don't, want a second dog.' Sally and I kept praying he would change his mind, and right up until the middle of January 2020, the answer remained, 'No'.

I was going to see the puppies at Sally's, around two weeks before they were old enough to go to their forever homes. On the Wednesday night I needed to have the conversation again with Darren about getting one of the puppies. I told him how I really wanted another dog as Coco was getting older, and she had given us so much joy that I felt it would be good for her to have a friend. Darren finally gave in and said, 'Yes!'

I went to meet the puppies the next day, and Sally had no idea that I was going to buy one. I had prayed before I got to her house, that the puppy that came to me and stayed with me, was the one I would choose. Most of the puppies came to meet me at the front door with their Mum, and as I entered. I asked, 'Which were the two boys that were still not sold?' To my delight, the tri-colour puppy following me was available. I picked him up and already had the name picked before I got there and announced to Sally that his name was Bear and I was buying him.

It took a long two weeks to wait before he was ready to come home, but finally, on the 3rd of February 2020 (eight weeks old), he came home and was introduced to Coco. Bear helped us cope with what was to come. God knew exactly the right time to bring Bear into our lives. I love that God knows us so intimately and knows just what we need and when we need it.

Life is totally different to what it was before.

Every day our Victorian Premier provided updates on the numbers that have tested positive for Covid 19 in the past 24 hours and the number of deaths caused by Covid 19 in the last 24 hours. We had army personnel on our streets going door-to-door checks on people who had tested positive. They were making sure these people were staying in their homes and isolating for a fourteen-day period.

Australia appeared to have done really well in containing the virus that had come in from overseas travellers. The first stage 3 lockdown, which lasted for three months, appeared to be working. What we saw from overseas was that this virus didn't discriminate between people groups or ages. The hospital adapted to the fast-moving changes that were happening. Initially, patients were only allowed two visitors a day. Visiting hours were restricted to two, two-hour time slots.

The first stage three lockdown began on the 31st of March 2020 and was in place for three months. Businesses closed, and workers worked from home. Restaurants were closed to people eating in; many adapted by offering takeaway only. Beauty salons (Taleisha's salon included) closed. Gyms closed. Clothing stores were also forced to close because they couldn't adhere to the four square meter rule that had been enforced.

The federal government developed a Job Seeker payment and Job Keeper scheme in order to help the thousands of people that found themselves unemployed. Fear and uncertainty were everywhere; no one was exempt. Churches closed as people were unable to physically meet together. Churches adapted by using technology and putting their services online. People connected together in zoom links. Cinemas closed, replaced by live stream television and Netflix. National parks closed, and even children's playgrounds closed. People were forced to stay home in an attempt to stop the virus from being transmitted from person to person.

People were told they had to maintain a 1.5-metre distance from each other. No more hugging and kissing each other when we met. For me, that was a challenging rule because I'm a very touchy-feely person.

As time went on, people's frustrations were boiling over. There were fights between people in the supermarkets over toilet paper and panic buying - people were only looking after themselves.

We had a total of six lockdowns.

During our sixth lockdown period, from the 5th of August 2021 to mid-September 2021, we found ourselves unable to connect physically with others, unable to visit family and friends or go to church as we were in stage 3 lockdown restrictions in regional Victoria.

Jordan and Taleisha, who were living in the Melbourne Metropolitan area, were in stage 4 lockdown – more severe restrictions. This meant that they couldn't go more than 5 kms from their house to exercise or shop. They could only go out to exercise for one hour a day. In both stages, there were only five reasons to leave your home - shopping for essential items, medical care, caregiving, exercise and work if you couldn't work from home. Home schooling was what many parents now found themselves doing. Schools and daycare centres were open only for children of essential workers, who couldn't home school their children.

I was nursing during this time, and the high levels of stress amongst staff was palpable. Each day at the hospital was different, with new protocols for how we did things. Situations changed rapidly on the wards. In the first wave of the pandemic, the hospital was preparing for the worst. We were seeing television footage of what was happening overseas; thousands were infected, and thousands were dying from this virus.

I personally had to take six weeks off due to the stress of the job. During my time off, I spent a lot of time leaning in, close to God, and drawing upon His love and strength. Just as I found after the fires, my God is faithful and always meets me where I am at. He has been my hope when the circumstances appeared hopeless, and His love has removed the fear.

Coco and Bear.

Chapter 16

Another 'New Normal'

Amongst all this, charities such as Big Group Hug and One Box were still operating to meet the ever-increasing needs for food and basic items. Big Group Hug is a charity run by volunteers that provides essential items, such as prams, cots, children's clothing and toiletries for women that have escaped from domestic violence and families struggling with being able to access the essential items that they need. These cases are referred through councils, councillors, social workers, churches and women's crisis centres.

I had joined Big Group Hug as a volunteer a year earlier. What drew me to this group was that they were practically helping families in need.

I remember the first time I walked around the warehouse and saw racks and racks of clothes and all sorts of donated goods. There were cots, prams, blankets, bed linen, nappies, toys, children's books and toiletries that had been all donated from companies and individuals.

I remember feeling totally overwhelmed; tears started to run down my cheeks. Memories flooded back of the relief centre that I had gone to after Black Saturday. I knew I wanted to be a part of this great organisation. I volunteered my time sorting children's clothing and toys and making up packs of children's clothes in various sizes that were required, including books and toys.

With every pack I made, I prayed that the family would be protected and blessed. I put a lot of effort into packing clothes for children. I wanted them to receive the best, just like my family had received after the fires. I know how humbling and hard it is to accept charity from others.

The Church I currently go to is Unihill Church in Bundoora. They purchased a warehouse a few years ago directly behind the Church building. It was called The Hope Centre. Now I look back, God definitely knew what he was doing and what was to come. Big Group Hug has been operating from The Hope Centre for around two years now.

The Churches Pastor for pastoral care is John Graham. He had been a part of the aid being organised through the Diamond Valley Baptist Church after Black Saturday. He was very aware of the needs of people and had the organisational skills to meet people's practical and spiritual needs.

A charity called One Box was already supplying boxes of food to people in need, so John organised to partner with them, and One Box was established in the Hope Centre, also run by volunteers. It started with thirty boxes of essential items such as bread, milk and fruit and vegetables. These went out to thirty families in need. The need in the community was so great, even before Covid 19, that John had to increase the boxes. He organised another thirty boxes of fruit and vegetables through a local fruit and vegetable store in Bundoora and called these *Fruit Boxes*.

The local fruiter packs the boxes with fruit and vegetables and then delivered them to the Hope Centre on Wednesdays, where volunteers, including me, added long-life milk and bread.

The bread was donated by a Brumbies bakery. The fruit boxes and long-life milk was donated by the church. When I heard about this earlier in the year, I knew immediately that I had to get involved with this wonderful charity as well.

During the first stage 3 lockdown, I was volunteering with One Box and Fruit Box in the morning on a Wednesday and then going next door to volunteer with Big Group Hug in the afternoon. Pastor John's vision for One Box and Fruit Box, was not only to feed people at this vulnerable time but also to meet spiritual needs, engaging with them as they pick up their boxes and finding out how they are going and letting them know that we are here for them.

My Father God never wastes any experience in our lives. He taught me so much on my short-term mission trips in Africa. I could draw on the things I had learned there, and after Black Saturday. I could also now draw on that experience to help others. I was coming from a position of understanding how people felt in their time of need.

Restrictions started to ease as it appeared we were getting on top of the Pandemic. After three months of stage 3 lockdown (31st of March 2020 – 1st of June 2020), businesses began to open up. Restaurants were able to take up to 20 people at a time, so long as their premises could keep to the strict 1.5-metre distance requirements.

Darren and I booked into our favourite restaurant in Thornbury as soon as we were able to dine in. It felt like such a luxury to dress up and go out for a meal. This was one of the things I had taken for granted - the freedom of going out and eating in at a restaurant. It was so exciting, coming back to our favourite restaurant. As was being able to go back to the gym, have waxing done at the beautician, and get your hair done - things that used to be normal routines now became so special. It reminded me again that our freedom to choose and do such simple things is so special.

Everyone was referring to getting back to some normality as the 'New Normal'. I had experienced this new Normal before, after the bushfires. Sometimes, life after a catastrophic event is never the same.

I'm reminded of the scripture John 10:10 (New International Version), 'The thief comes only to steal and kill and destroy, I have come that you may have life, and have it to the full.'

We had around three weeks of relative freedom in Victoria. Suddenly the numbers affected by Covid 19 started going up in the hundreds. We were now seeing deaths every 24 hours. Once more, the television was reporting increasing numbers. It appeared Victoria was now being hit by a second wave of the virus.

Nursing homes had a large number of transmissions and casualties. Medical staff were being put under immense pressure in our hospitals. To protect staff and patients, no visitors were allowed in the hospital. It appeared to be a freight train, speeding out of control. Melbourne Metropolitan Area was again placed into Stage 4 restrictions, from Sunday the 2nd of August 2020 to the 28th of October 2020.

Now Jordan and Taleisha and other family and friends living in the Melbourne Metropolitan area were again forced into even tighter restrictions. More businesses shut down, even parts of the building industry, to try and slow the spread of the virus, by restricting people's movements.

In addition to the previous stage 4 restrictions being re-imposed, a curfew was also implemented between 8 pm and 5 am. People had to carry permits for going beyond the 5 km radius to work or any essential appointments.

There was more unemployment due to stricter business closures. The Victorian border was totally shut down to all other states. Army and Police checkpoints were set up at all interstate borders. There were also, lines separating Melbourne Metropolitan areas and rural areas. The media showed scenes of absolute panic and chaos with people trying to get across the borders before they were closed. If people didn't get across the border before the deadline, they would be forced to self-quarantine in a hotel for fourteen days at their own expense. Again, fear and uncertainty played out in people's lives.

I lived in Kinglake, which is classed as rural, so at the time we were under stage 3 restrictions. We didn't have a curfew like Melbourne, but everything again been shut down, including gyms, restaurants, pubs, and beauticians. We were not allowed any visitors in our home. I was unable to visit my children, family or friends in Melbourne, and they would be fined if they came up to Kinglake.

We continued to connect via Facetime and Zoom. Our church services were live-streamed on YouTube. This way, we were at least praying together and staying connected. We hadn't been able to meet together as a church family, since the end of March 2020, in the first stage 3 lockdown.

No one knew when we would be able to finally travel interstate from Victoria, which made us feel very disconnected from the whole country. There was no certainty when international travel would be allowed again.

Through all this uncertainty, I just placed my faith and hope in my Heavenly Father, knowing that He knows the beginning and the end. He has always been faithful to me, and my family and I had no reason to doubt His faithfulness then.

Chapter 17

Where Are We Now?

Who was to know that the Covid 19 pandemic would continue to have its grip on us even into 2022.

The Victorian premier has now removed a lot of the previous restrictions, and businesses have reopened. Borders to other states in Australia have reopened, but there are still different rules for the different states regarding isolation rules for people coming in and those who have COVID and who are close contacts.

Darren and I are still reluctant to travel interstate due to the continued uncertainty of border restrictions.

The pandemic is still causing divisions with people. Now we have those that have chosen to be vaccinated and those that have chosen not to be. Governments are imposing restrictions on the unvaccinated such as, not allowing them to dine in at restaurants or cafes, or attend sporting venues such as gyms and wedding reception venues. Again the different states of Australia have different rules for vaccinated and unvaccinated people.

This has caused a lot of anger and fear in the community. People feel discriminated against. Families are divided over choices that individuals have made. Governments have even made vaccinations mandatory for various workplaces such as hospitality staff, teachers, nurses, doctors, anyone working in a hospital, aged care workers, paramedics, shop workers, hotel workers and pilots and airline workers. Thousands of nurses and people in these other industries have lost their jobs due to them choosing not to have the vaccinations.

There have been personal challenges as well during the pandemic. I received a phone call from Dad and Mum in late August 2021, asking if I would come to Korumburra to take Dad for an urgent biopsy on a lesion that had developed in his leg. Regional areas such as Kinglake and Korumburra were under stage 3 lockdown at the time. Dad had arranged for me to have a letter from his local GP to say that I was coming as a carer to take Dad to his appointment. At the time, we were unable to travel throughout Victoria, and Melbourne was under even stricter lockdown rules. Because we hadn't been able to visit for many months due to lockdowns, I was shocked when I saw the state Dad was in, both physically and mentally.

At the beginning of the pandemic, Dad had been diagnosed with cancer. In early March 2020, Dad was taken to St Vincents Hospital in Melbourne for urgent surgery on his leg, and he began his chemotherapy treatment. Fortunately, I was still able to freely go into the hospital with Mum to see him.

The Friday he was discharged home, I was able to go to Korumburra and help Mum settle him and then at midnight that Friday night Victoria was plunged into its first big lockdown. This meant I was unable to travel and support Mum by nursing Dad through this very difficult challenge in our family's lives. Dad had to make his chemotherapy journey alone, as Mum was not allowed to go into the hospital to sit with him and support him during his treatments.

There were many facetime calls over the next 18 months. Darren and I got a very small window of opportunity to go and see Mum and Dad when regional Victoria was able to move around but still not able to go into Melbourne without a valid reason. So we were still unable to see family members living in Melbourne, and they were unable to visit us in regional Victoria.

The biopsy was to reveal that the cancer was back and as Dad's local GP said, 'It was very aggressive.' I stayed and helped Mum nurse Dad at home for as long as we could. His condition was deteriorating rapidly, so an ambulance was called to take him to the hospital. At the time, hospitals had a no visitor policy due to COVID 19. Dad's condition was deteriorating so rapidly that the hospital allowed Mum, my brother Max and me to go in at any time of the day or night. I was able to nurse him in what turned out to be his final days, which is a time I really cherish.

A few days later, after speaking with the doctors, we had to make the heartbreaking decision to make Dad's care palliative as there was nothing more that could be done medically. I remember walking in a nearby park with Mum, tears rolling down my face, saying it wasn't fair that Dad was dying during COVID, where no one was allowed to visit him, not even his brothers and sisters. His funeral could only have ten people present, which turned out to be just our immediate family members.

Dad was a man who had touched so many lives with the love of God. He was a leader in churches he had attended and ministered to many people over his life with his gift of music. He was always the first to offer his help to anyone who needed it. One of my first questions to the funeral director was whether they could arrange the service to be live-streamed. Dad had touched so many people's lives that many people wanted to be present at his funeral and couldn't due to the COVID restrictions. At least this was a way people could participate in celebrating his life.

Dad passed away peacefully on Thursday the 2nd of September 2021. Mum and I were with him, and he flew out of our arms straight into the arms of Jesus. I was so thankful that we could be there with him at the end. On the 9th of September, we honoured Dad's life in a very intimate funeral service at the funeral home's chapel. Although only the immediate family was present, the service was viewed by hundreds of people via the live stream. I am so grateful that Dad passed away peacefully in the end, and we were able to share via live stream with his many family and friends. Celebrating a life that was so well lived.

Right now, Darren and I are still living in Kinglake in the house we rebuilt on our original block of land. Darren has started a new company called Aztek Wind and Solar. He installs and designs solar systems with his business partner, Aaron. An offshoot of Aztek is Aztek Motorcycles, where they restore older Ducati's and sell them.

I have just resigned from my nursing position at the Austin Hospital after 22 years of service. I am still volunteering at One Box (Food Pantry) and Big Group Hug. I have been painting as well as doing pottery, tapping into my creative side. After 36 years in a nursing career, I'm unsure of what the next stage of my life will look like, but I'm excited to see what it is and what it will look like. My boys are both married and embarking on the next stages of their lives. Darren and I are empty nesters now.

The community of Kinglake feels very different now. Initially, around a quarter of the community didn't return after the fire. Many of those who did rebuild or buy homes that had been spared by the fire have sold up and moved from the area, and new people have moved in. I don't see as many of the original residents around the town, so this is very different. Initially, I found these changes really hard because the sense of close community had shifted. The realisation that the new people didn't have that understanding of the effects of the fire on the area was also initially difficult to accept.

As the years have gone on, I have made new friendships through the gym and various art activities through the Kinglake Rangers Neighbourhood House. New people into the area have brought with them fresh ideas, and new businesses have been formed in Kinglake. Seasons change, and I find myself changing with them.

Samuel, our youngest son, is now 24 years old. He has just begun his motor mechanic apprenticeship with My Car. On the 20th of March, Samuel was married to his beautiful fiance, Madison. On that day, he became a stepdad to her son Andy. It's wonderful to watch the bond Samuel and Andy already had.

Jordan and Taleisha are living down in Mernda. Jordan is the operations pastor at Unihill Church two days a week. He is also working for a not-for-profit organisation called Open House, which helps underprivileged families, youth and the elderly. He works for Open House three days a week. He is now 30 years old, and he and Taleisha have been married for four years now. Time has definitely flown since their wedding in the paddock. Taleisha is working as a beautician at Beauty on Walnut in Whittlesea. Just after Easter 2022, Jordan and Taleisha announced that they were expecting a baby, which has brought so much excitement and joy to Darren and me.

Coco is now 12 years old. Bear is two years old, and they both bring so much joy to our lives. Even as I'm writing, Coco and Bear are sitting with me, keeping me company.

Through it all, God has shown me His faithfulness. Even living in this time of the unknown, I know He is with me. I hold onto these scriptures.

> 'For I know the thoughts and plans that I have for you, says the Lord, thoughts and plans for welfare and peace and not evil. To give you hope in your final outcome.' *Jeremiah 29:11 (Amplified)*

> 'God is faithful (Reliable, Trustworthy, and therefore ever true to His promise, and He can be depended on); by Him, you were called into companionship and participation with His Son, Jesus Christ our Lord.' *1 Corinthians 1:9 (Amplified)*

This journey for the past thirteen years has been full of trials and triumphs. It has shown me how much family and friends matter and that you never know what tomorrow may bring, so live and appreciate every day. I have learnt not to hold too tightly to things but to appreciate the relationships around you.

It doesn't matter what situation you're facing, be it fire, floods, divorce or loss of a loved one, there is always hope. My faith has been an integral part of my journey of recovery. You can get through anything if you don't give up hope.

Samuel and Madison's wedding.

Samuel and Madison.

Samuel with Andy.

Our home now.

About Me

My name is Bronwyn Wakelin

I was born in Melbourne on the 18th of November 1965.

On the 7th of February 2009 my life changed forever.

I live in Kinglake, Victoria and I'm a survivor of the Black Saturday bush fires in 2009, along with my husband Darren and two amazing boys, Jordan and Samuel.

I have been dreaming of publishing my story. It has been a work in progress over the last four years.

When I initially started writing it at the beginning of 2018, I had to put the pen down as I began to completely unravel.

With the help of a psychologist, family, my Church family, friends and my faith I was gradually able to climb out of the blackness and continue to write my story. It has been quite an amazing process, and I have seen God's hand in every step.

Just after the 10th Anniversary of Black Saturday, I was contacted by a journalist who wanted to interview me and put my story in the *Take 5* magazine. She had also authored her own books.

Over the next few years she encouraged and mentored me in writing my story. Unfortunately, she was unable to take me through the publishing process, but I'm so thankful for her help and encouragement up to that point.

I was speaking with another friend and she told me to contact Antoinette Pellegrini who was an author, mentor and editor and could guide me through the publishing process. From the moment we met, Antoinette and I had an instant affinity and have fast become friends through the process. I love how the Lord knows exactly who you need to connect with at a specific time.

The aim of publishing my story is to encourage others that there is always hope, even in situations that appear to be hopeless.

I was married in April 1985 to Darren, my soulmate and best friend.

We have two amazing boys, Jordan and Samuel, and now two amazing daughters-in-law, one beautiful three-year-old grandson and another grandchild on the way, due in November 2022.

I am a registered nurse of 36 years and love volunteering with my Church and various community groups.

I believe everyone has a story to tell, and this is mine.

Bronwyn Wakelin